IMAGES
of America

THE BAYOUS
OF HOUSTON

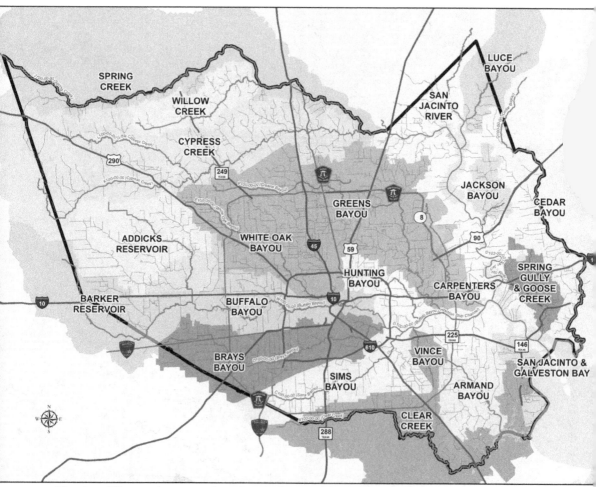

The city of Houston lies primarily within the limits of Harris County. Twenty-two major watersheds drain the county. The major bayou or creek within each watershed has helped shape the growth of Houston. (Courtesy of HCFCD.)

ON THE COVER: During the 1935 flood, Buffalo Bayou was 52 feet above normal level and reached the bottom of the Main Street Viaduct. Other bridges, such as the Capitol Avenue High Bridge, were completely submerged. Traffic in the downtown was disrupted for days, and it took months to repair buildings that were flooded. (Courtesy of HCFCD.)

IMAGES
of America

THE BAYOUS
OF HOUSTON

James L. Sipes and Matthew K. Zeve

ARCADIA
PUBLISHING

Published by Arcadia Publishing
Charleston, South Carolina

Library of Congress Control Number: 2012949220

For all general information, please contact Arcadia Publishing:
Telephone 843-853-2070
Fax 843-853-0044
E-mail sales@arcadiapublishing.com
For customer service and orders:
Toll-Free 1-888-313-2665

Visit us on the Internet at www.arcadiapublishing.com

*Special thanks to the Harris County Flood Control District
and all of the organizations, agencies, and individuals that are
dedicated to protecting and enhancing the bayous of Houston.*

CONTENTS

ACKNOWLEDGMENTS

The authors would like to thank Noah Taylor for his continuous support and encouragement during the development of this book. We would also like to thank Ed Lyden and David Valentin at Harris County Flood Control District, and the rest of the HCFCD staff for their support.

INTRODUCTION

Houston has been known as the "Bayou City" ever since it was first established in 1836. When brothers August C. and John K. Allen were looking for a location for a new town, they selected a site at the confluence of Buffalo Bayou and White Oak Bayou. They were looking to create an inland port, and this location was the westernmost navigable point. Ever since then, Houston and its bayous have been indelibly linked.

Growth of the city was tied directly to the bayous—specifically Buffalo Bayou—which have provided the lifeblood of Houston. There are over 2,500 miles of waterways in Harris County, and they are as much a part of Houston as its buildings, roads, and parks. Almost all of the early development occurred along Buffalo Bayou. As soon as docks were built along the bayou in 1836, business started, and it is still going strong. The Allen brothers immediately started marketing in order to entice settlers to come to their new town. They named it after Gen. Sam Houston, the hero of the Battle of San Jacinto who was expected to be the first president of Texas. Advertisements in newspapers helped convince people to come to the new town, and almost overnight, Houston was born.

The bayous have been good to Houston. It is the largest city in the state of Texas and the fourth largest city in the United States. The Houston metropolitan area is home to 5.4 million people, a far cry from the dozen people who lived in Houston when it was first founded. The Port of Houston ranks first in the country in foreign tonnage and is the sixth-largest port in the world. A problem, though, is that as Houston has grown and expanded, the bayous have been seriously impacted.

Harris County has 22 major watersheds that each drain into 22 major waterways. Watersheds in the Houston Area include Addicks Reservoir, Armand Bayou, Barker Reservoir, Brays Bayou, Buffalo Bayou, Carpenters Bayou, Cedar Bayou, Clear Creek, Cypress Creek, Galveston Bay, Greens Bayou, Halls Bayou, Hunting Bayou, Jackson Bayou, Luce Bayou; San Jacinto River, Sims Bayou, Spring Creek, Spring Gully/Goose Creek, Vince Bayou, White Oak Bayou, and Willow Creek. Although there are 2,500 miles of waterways in Harris County, only around 800 miles of natural channels were in the county when Houston was founded. The rest have been added over the years to improve drainage and allow for development. Almost all of the manmade and improved channels were built prior to establishing the criteria of the one percent (100-year) flood.

The watersheds vary in size and complexity, but each has its own problems in terms of growth and development, flooding, water quality, and recreation and environmental concerns. Many of the bayous have been widened, paved, cleared of native vegetation, dredged, and encroached upon by development. The US Army Corps of Engineers, Harris County Flood Control District, City of Houston, and other agencies have invested more than $4 billion to create a network of flood damage reduction elements in an attempt to reduce flooding. The result has been a loss of wildlife habitat, water quality, and ecological sustainability. Urban stormwater runoff has contaminated the bayous to a point where they have been significantly impacted.

Prior to human settlement, the bayous of Houston were very different than they are now. Originally, most were overgrown with vegetation, lined with trees along the banks, and set in areas with native woodlands or grasslands. Wildlife was abundant because the combination of water and vegetative cover made for a perfect habitat. The bayous flooded when it rained because the channels were typically fairly small, the existing vegetation would have slowed down stormwater flow, and the surrounding terrain was relatively flat. But it was not a problem when the bayous flooded because that was part of the natural environment. Approximately 25–35 percent of Harris County lies within the 100-year flood plain, and these are the areas that commonly flood.

Despite all of the engineering to Houston's bayous, the region still floods frequently during heavy rainfall. Every time there is a storm or hurricane there are floods, and the results can be catastrophic. For example, when Tropical Storm Allison hit in 2001, it flooded more than 73,000 homes and caused billions of dollars in damages. Twenty people lost their lives.

Many Houston residents believe that the bayous are a critical part of the city, and future growth of the city must be in sync with efforts to improve the bayous, reduce negative impacts, and restore them to a point where they are ecologically sustainable. Projects such as the Buffalo Bayou Park, Buffalo Bayou Promenade, the Rosemont Bridge over Buffalo Bayou, Sims Bayou Federal Flood Damage Reduction Project, Stude Park, Sesquicentennial Park, Terry Hershey Park, Edith L. Moore Nature Sanctuary, Project Brays, Brays Bayou Tidal Marsh Project, Greens Bayou Wetlands Mitigation Bank, and the Arthur Storey Park Stormwater Detention Basin are just a few examples of projects along the bayous that seek to improve their visual and environmental quality.

One

PRIOR TO 1836
EARLY SETTLEMENTS

Early French and Spanish explorers visited the area in the 1600s through the 1700s, but few stayed. The land was scattered with grasses and wooded forests, and the bayous provided the water needed to support natural habitat for flora and fauna. Explorers followed the bayous and used them for navigation as well as a source of water. In the centuries before European explorers visited the region, Native Americans camped and hunted in the area and fished along the banks of the bayous. It was not until the 1820s that European explorers established settlements along the bayou. In 1803, the United States obtained the Louisiana Purchase from Napoleon.

Settlers started moving into the area in the early 1800s. In the 1820s, Stephen F. Austin encouraged American settlers to come to Texas. Austin had a land grant, originally obtained by his father, which allowed 300 American families to "settle in southeast Texas," and some of these settlers used the bayous for travel. Neighboring Galveston was the first European settlement in the region, having been founded in 1816, and Harrisburg was established in 1825 a few miles away on the banks of Buffalo Bayou. The west side of Galveston Island included a natural, deepwater harbor, but it was difficult to get to the island from mainland Texas.

The 1820s and 1830s were decades of change in Texas. In 1821, Mexico declared its independence from Spain, and Texas became a Mexican province. Anglo-American settlers moving into the territory soon outnumbered the Mexicans. In 1830, Mexican officials passed a law prohibiting further American immigration, which led to dissent among the Americans.

In the Brazos River valley, northwest of the current location of Houston, plantations produced mountains of cotton, and it was important to find a way to get these crops to Galveston where they could be loaded on ships and sent to markets in New York and London. Buffalo Bayou was the major body of water that connected the Brazos River plantations to Galveston Bay.

Buffalo Bayou is one of the longest bayous in the Houston area at 53 miles in length. The Buffalo Bayou watershed covers approximately 103 square miles and has about 116 miles of open streams within the watershed. Although the watershed has been almost completely urbanized, some of the banks still look much like they did before human settlement. These photographs show Buffalo Bayou, just east of the city. (Both, courtesy of HCFCD.)

Buffalo Bayou's natural geology consists of a mix of sandy, silty, and clay banks that erode doing periods when the water overflows the banks. Flooding was a natural part of the bayou ecosystem, and the Buffalo Bayou corridor would have looked much like this in the days before human settlement. The bottom of the bayou is muddy and silty, so the channel would have shifted over the years. (Courtesy of HCDCD.)

The Brays Bayou watershed, which is 31 miles long and covers approximately 127 square miles, is located in southwest Harris County and portions of Ft. Bend County. Historical records indicate that before the establishment of Houston, Brays Bayou was a small, meandering stream clogged with natural vegetation and lined on both sides with trees, with sandbars along the inside of the bayou bends because of the slow-moving water. (Courtesy of HCFCD.)

The White Oak Bayou watershed is located in central Harris County. The bayou joins Buffalo Bayou in downtown Houston. The watershed covers about 111 square miles and includes three primary streams: White Oak Bayou, Little White Oak Bayou, and Cole Creek. There are about 151 miles of open streams in the White Oak Bayou watershed. (Courtesy of HCFCD.)

Two

1836–1869

FOUNDING OF HOUSTON

When Gen. Sam Houston defeated the Mexican army at the Battle of San Jacinto on April 21, 1936, Texas independence was established. That same year, settlers August and John Allen founded a new city at the confluence of Buffalo and White Oak Bayous, and named it after General Houston.

Buffalo Bayou was the lifeline of the new town, providing a means of shipping and transportation as well as serving as a focal point for development.

When Houston was first established, Buffalo Bayou was a shallow, narrow waterway overgrown with vegetation and blocked by sandbars and downed trees. Skeptics wondered if the bayou could be used for navigation and transportation. To promote the idea of Houston as a shipping port, the Allen Brothers hired the steamship *Laura*, owned by the shipping firm of McKinney and Williams, to travel from Galveston Bay to Houston. The 16-mile trip took three days to complete. In 1937, the Allen brothers brought the 150-foot *Constitution* to Houston, but there was no room for the steamship to turn around, so it was forced to back up to what is now called the "Turning Basin."

The new town took off, and hundreds of people moved to Houston. Most of Houston's original settlers came on small boats up the bayou. For two years, from 1837 to 1839, Houston was the capital of the republic of Texas before it was moved to Austin.

Shortly after the new settlement was established, it flooded, and Houston's new residents had to walk around for days in knee-deep water. Efforts were made to drain the swampy land in order to convert it into a suitable site for a city. Yellow fever was a major problem; in 1839, the disease killed about 12 percent of the population. In 1841, a storm lasting two days flooded the city and washed out bridges on Buffalo Bayou. Two years later, flooding occurred on Buffalo, White Oak, and Brays Bayous. In 1845, Texas became a state. Three years later, the Mexican-American War ended, and Houston was on the edge of a new horizon.

The original map for the city of Houston was based upon a grid pattern that created city blocks south of Buffalo Bayou. The Allen brothers commissioned the map, which was created by Gail Borden. The angle of the grid is based on that of the bayou, so each major street extends to the bayou. (Courtesy Special Collections, University of Houston Libraries, UH Digital Library.)

Changes happened quickly during Houston's first decade. On January 1, 1837, the town comprised 12 residents and one log cabin; four months later, there were 1,500 people and 100 houses. The Allen brothers greatly exaggerated the merits of Houston in order to entice settlers to move to the new town, as the mountains in this engraving illustrate. The city was made the capital of the Republic of Texas for a short time, until it was shifted to Austin in 1839. Texas became the 28th state of the Union in 1845. Although it still had difficulties, people continued to move to the fledgling bayou town, and in 1850, the population was 2,396. (Courtesy Special Collections, University of Houston Libraries, UH Digital Library.)

This map shows Texas in 1841. The areas along the coast were starting to grow, but much of the rest of the state was very much a frontier. In 1841, the mayor of Houston established the Port of Houston, which was supported by the city and later by the state of Texas. (Courtesy of HCFCD.)

The city of Houston was named after Gen. Sam Houston, the popular war hero of the Battle of San Jacinto, where the Texian Army defeated Gen. Antonio López de Santa Anna's Mexican forces. Apparently, the Allen brothers believed that General Houston was assured of being the first elected president of Texas. The marketing ploy was a smart one, because General Houston was elected president, and his popularity may indeed have helped "sell" the idea of a new city along Buffalo Bayou.

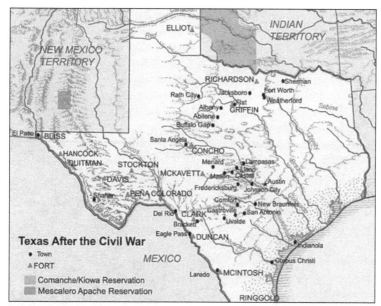

By 1860, 4,845 people resided in Houston. There were no Civil War battles that occurred in Houston, but the war did have a significant, indirect impact on the town and the region. The war effort and the consequent dislocation of people left the entire state of Texas in economic devastation. Four years of military rule after the end of the war greatly limited growth in Houston during that time.

French artist E. Therond took some liberties when he created this engraving of what is supposed to be Houston in 1859. The illustration looks more like a quaint mountain village in the French Alps than the emerging city of Houston. Anyone who has been to Houston knows there are no mountains anywhere in the region. According to the University of Houston's Special Collections Library, this engraving may have been based on an 1840s sketch of Houston made by a British artist. It appeared in *L'Illustration* and was used by land speculators in Europe to attract entrepreneurs and investors to Houston. (Courtesy of Special Collections, University of Houston Libraries, UH Digital Library.)

Three

1870–1899
COMPETING WITH GALVESTON

The big news in 1870 was that Texas was readmitted to the Union. After the end of the Civil War, Texas had been under Presidential Reconstruction and then under Congressional Reconstruction. The state was required to conduct a constitutional convention that led to a new state constitution providing for universal adult male suffrage. Once the new constitution was approved, Texas was again a part of the United States of America.

Between 1870 and 1899, Houston continued to grow, but it still played second fiddle to Galveston, which was the largest and most successful city in Texas. The competition between the two cities seemed to spur development in both. In 1870, Congress designated Houston as a port of delivery, and the US Army Corps of Engineers initiated a survey of the Houston Ship Channel. The study was completed in 1871, and the corps presented design recommendations for improved navigation. Efforts were made to widen and dredge portions of the bayous. By 1876, the waterway was clear enough for the steamship *Clinton* to navigate all the way to Sims Bayou. As a result of these types of improvements, there was heavy steamship and schooner travel into Houston during the 1880s and 1890s. In addition, Houston's Union Station opened in 1880, and by the end of the century, the city was known as the Railroad Capital of Texas.

A hurricane hit Galveston in 1875, and portions of Houston flooded. In addition, a major storm hit the White Oak and Buffalo Bayou areas in 1879, resulting in significant flooding. The floods made national headlines.

Houston's municipal waterworks opened in 1879. This was important for the continued growth of the city because the water in Buffalo Bayou was so polluted by trash and industrial waste. To help address these types of problems, the Rivers and Harbors Appropriation Act was passed in 1899. This act, the oldest federal environmental law, makes it a misdemeanor to discharge any type of refuse into navigable waters or to excavate, fill, or dam any part of the water body.

This 1884 photograph shows Main Street in downtown Houston. By 1890, a thriving Houston had approximately 27,500 residents, and the feeling was that the city was quickly moving into the modern age. Streets were being paved with block or cobblestone, electric lights illuminated the city, Union Station was always busy, and Houston was viewed as the Railroad Capital of Texas. Galveston was still the largest and wealthiest city in Texas, but Houston was gaining. (Courtesy of Special Collections, University of Houston Libraries, UH Digital Library.)

In 1970, Congress designated Houston a port of delivery. Galveston was still the largest city in Texas as well as the biggest port, but Houston was a popular port because it linked to railroad lines that made it easier to transport goods. This view of Houston is from a point north of Buffalo Bayou. (Courtesy of Special Collections, University of Houston Libraries, UH Digital Library.)

Horse-drawn rigs were all the rage in Houston during the 1890s. These streetcars helped improve access in the downtown area. Eventually, these types of streetcars were replaced after the first automobile arrived in Houston around 1900. By 1904, there were more than 80 vehicles in the city. (Courtesy of HCFCD.)

Passengers climb aboard the *Ethel B. Houston* ferry at the historic Allen's Landing in downtown Houston. During this time, there was heavy steamship and schooner travel into Houston. By the middle of the decade, a dozen steamships and 22 schooners were scheduling daily voyages from Allen's Landing. With the popularity of water travel, there was an increasing demand for a deep-water ship channel in Houston. (Courtesy of HCFCD.)

In the South, the term "King Cotton" was used liberally, because ever since the first cotton plantation was established in Texas in 1822, cotton has been a dominant crop. The crop was shipped overland from across the state and then loaded into barges, such as the *Jackson* (pictured in this 1899 photograph), which moved down Buffalo Bayou and the Ship Channel to waiting steamers and then shipped to markets worldwide. Between 1854 and 1860, the volume of cotton shipped from Houston nearly tripled, and that trend continued into the next century. (Courtesy of HCFCD.)

This 1890 photograph shows a large pavilion in Magnolia Park, which is located along Buffalo Bayou. Magnolia Park is a neighborhood that was established in 1890 on 1,374 acres near the Houston Ship Channel in eastern Harris County. The neighborhood was named for the 3,750 magnolias that developers planted on the site. It is considered one of Houston's oldest Hispanic neighborhoods because many of the Mexican Americans arriving from South Texas around 1911 settled in the area. (Courtesy of Special Collections, University of Houston Libraries, UH Digital Library.)

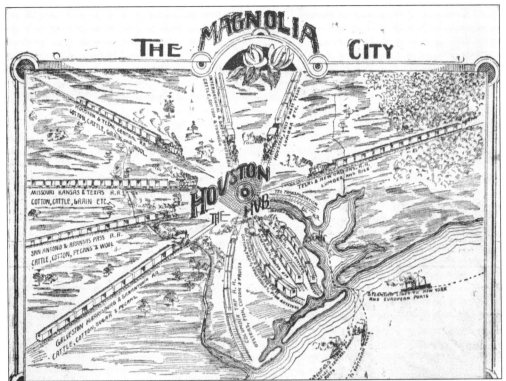

This map, entitled *The Manufacturing and Distributing Point of Texas*, depicts trains from all over the region coming into Houston and then being distributed via steamboats north to New York and European ports and south to Central American and Mexican ports. The extension of railroads into the state paralleled the growth of commercial centers in major regions and an increase in cotton, livestock, and lumber production. This map was printed in the *Texas World* newspaper. (Courtesy of Special Collections, University of Houston Libraries, UH Digital Library.)

The Houston Heights Hotel was built on the comer of Nineteenth and Ashland Streets in the late 1890s. It was destroyed by fire on June 1, 1915. At the time of this 1898 photograph, the hotel exemplified the economic growth and optimism that was part of the Houston culture. Around this time, room and board ran about $3.50 per week. (Courtesy of Special Collections, University of Houston Libraries, UH Digital Library.)

This series of maps, developed by A.L. Westyard, show Houston in 1891. The original grid pattern that was put in place in 1836 is still evident and has been expanded to accommodate the rapid growth of the city. Buffalo Bayou can be seen meandering through the middle. Along the bottom of the map, Westyard illustrates some of the major buildings in Houston at the time, and the variety of buildings reflects the diversity. They housed hotels, railroad stations, banks, retail stores, manufacturing, and oil, gas, and other related service industries. In many ways, the rivalry with Galveston spurred growth in Houston, as the competition led to a continued modernization of the city.

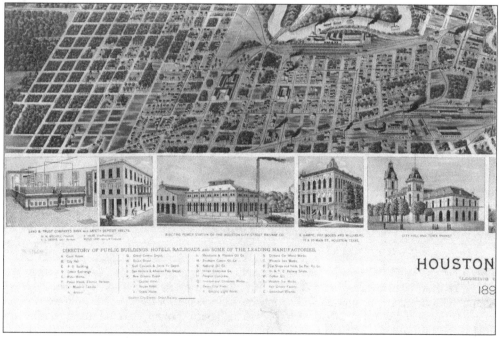

Flooding was still a problem in Houston. In 1879, the Bayou City suffered a massive flood along both Buffalo and White Oak Bayous. The *New York Times* article "Floods in Texas" noted, "the water rose 18 feet in three hours and carried away all the railroad bridges and many warehouses." Many buildings were submerged, and the residents were driven out. In early 1891, many of the streets along Buffalo Bayou were flooded as a result of intense rainfall that left Main Street completely underwater. Until the late 1880s, the bayou was the source of the city's drinking water, and water quality was constantly an issue. In 1887, two artesian wells were drilled. Bayou water was then only used for fighting fires. There were also concerns about the sanitary conditions of the city. On July 3, 1889, the *Galveston Daily News* wrote, "Everybody is kicking about the terrifying sanitary condition of the city, and fear that there will be a good deal of sickness unless the city authorities come to the front and have some cleaning up done."

This engraving shows the International & Great Northern Railroad Bridge over Buffalo Bayou in 1890. The railroad was created in 1873 and at its peak owned more than 1,100 miles of track. Railroads like the International & Great Northern allowed farmers, ranchers, and miners throughout the South to ship goods to Houston where they were loaded on steamers. It was this combination of rail and ship that allowed Houston to become a major hub of activity. (Courtesy of Special Collections, University of Houston Libraries, UH Digital Library.)

This 1890 photograph shows people disembarking from railcars among the trees in Magnolia Park on the south bank of Buffalo Bayou near Houston. John Thomas Brady owned the property that was developed into Magnolia Park. He also owned the Houston Belt and Magnolia Park Railway, which was where the Houston public flocked for picnics and other outdoor events. (Courtesy of Special Collections, University of Houston Libraries, UH Digital Library.)

Four

1900–1909

Galveston Storm, Spindletop, and Ship Channel

Three events that occurred during this period had a dramatic impact on the future of Houston. The first, in September 1900, was a hurricane and subsequent storm surge that hit Galveston Island, all but wiping out the City of Galveston. Till this point, Galveston was the largest and most successful city in Texas, but it never fully recovered from the disaster. The balance of commercial activity shifted, and future economic growth in the region focused on Houston.

The second event was a major gusher at Spindletop near Beaumont in 1901, which helped make Texas the national leader in the oil industry and Houston the hub of oil refining and distribution. Oil companies moved to Houston in droves.

The third event occurred in 1902, when the US government and the city of Houston reached an agreement to construct the Houston Ship Channel. Widening and dredging the Buffalo Bayou and Galveston Bay would make Houston a deepwater port, opening up new opportunities for shipping.

Downtown Houston was undergoing some major changes as well. The city's first skyscraper was constructed in 1906, and the increasing popularity of automobiles raised concerns about the need for paved streets. There were only a handful of automobiles in the early 1900s, but there were 1,031 in Harris County in 1911 and 97,902 by 1930. In 1900, the city constructed the first of what would be many paved streets. This was an effort to "get Houston out of the mud," which was a popular statement at the time.

Growth in Houston and adjacent areas had a major impact on the bayous. Much of the native woodlands around the bayous were cut down to accommodate new developments, and there were concerns about water quality and the loss of wildlife habitat. Much of Houston's basic infrastructure was in place during this time.

By the turn of the 20th century, Houston was a small, progressive city of around 45,000 people. Downtown Houston was undergoing significant changes, with two- and three-story structures giving way to taller buildings. Construction of the city's first skyscrapers, such as the 13-story Union National Bank Building and 11-story Scanlan Building, completely changed the Houston skyline. By 1910, Houston had grown to 78,800, in large part due to the decline of Galveston. (Courtesy of Special Collections, University of Houston Libraries, UH Digital Library.)

This engraving shows Buffalo Bayou in 1900. In 1870, The US Army Corps of Engineers surveyed the Buffalo Bayou channel and developed design recommendations. The bayou was widened and deepened in 1900, and shortly thereafter, the US government and Houston agreed to split the cost of transforming the eastern section of Buffalo Bayou into the Houston Ship Channel. (Courtesy of Special Collections, University of Houston Libraries, UH Digital Library.)

When oil was discovered at Spindletop in 1901, Houston's economy changed almost overnight. Spindletop is located near Beaumont, 90 miles northeast of Houston. It was not the first oil discovered in Texas, but it was the start of the oil boom within the state. Over the next few years, Texas became a national leader in the oil industry, and Houston became known as an oil town. Up until that time, Houston's economy was largely based on agriculture and ranching, and cotton, cattle, timber, rice, and fish were the most commonly produced products. Houston quickly became the oil refining and distribution destination for Spindletop as well as for other major oil fields in the region. By 1906, some 30 oil companies had opened offices within the city. (Courtesy of Special Collections, University of Houston Libraries, UH Digital Library.)

On September 8, 1900, the Great Storm of 1900 hit Galveston. The city was devastated by hurricane winds of more than 100 miles per hour and a 15-foot storm surge that literally destroyed the city. More than 5,000 people died, thousands more were left homeless, and very few buildings on the island were left standing. Up until that point, Galveston was considered to be one of the wealthiest and most successful cities in the country. (Courtesy of the Library of Congress.)

After the storm, many of the survivors decided to move elsewhere, and Galveston was no longer considered the commercial capital of the southwest. Houston escaped most of the damage that hit Galveston, and it quickly became the major port in Texas. Unlike Galveston, the Port of Houston is located inland and is not as exposed to hurricane storm surges. (Courtesy of the Library of Congress.)

This postcard shows downtown Houston's Congress Avenue around 1860 or 1870. Louis van Meldert sent the card to relatives in Belgium. Translated, it reads, "My dear Olive. Yesterday, the weather was very hot. Today, it is very cold. Vandenbrook has been in bed for 10 days, very sick. Me, I have influenza and rheumatisms in my whole left side. However, I have to walk to Middleham Castle. Do not bring the objects I had announced to you. They will probably leave by the Farnham. I will let you know. Since my last letter is no longer in my bed. These are some quick news. Kiss everyone for me. You as well, Leon." (Translated by Claude Chiasson. Courtesy www.baytownlibrary.org.)

The image on this postcard, labeled "Bayou City cotton compress," shows a loaded barge on Buffalo Bayou near Houston's Main Street viaduct. The card reads, "My dear Louis, I believed you to be in pension [boarding school] and I was totally charmed to learn my dear nephew was taking care of your mathematics. Thank him for me. Leon." (Translated by Claude Chiasson. Courtesy www.baytownlibrary.org.)

This 1909 postcard shows a boat on Buffalo Bayou's Long Reach. The two-and-a-half-mile stretch of bayou runs along Magnolia Park, and the proximity to the park has helped minimize development and protect the mixture of deciduous trees, shrubs, and groundcover along both sides of the bayou. (Courtesy of Special Collections, University of Houston Libraries, UH Digital Library.)

The 1900 Galveston Storm was actually a category four hurricane, and it devastated Galveston Island. Most of the island's buildings, which were primarily wood structures, were leveled. This image of a young boy sitting on a pile of debris was typical of what could be seen on any part of the island. (Courtesy of the Library of Congress.)

In 1900, Houston was a city in transition. On January 1, 1900, the *Galveston Daily News* wrote a long editorial on the many merits of Galveston harbor as the "chief harbor of the Texas coast." The article outlined the virtues that made Galveston the city of the future for the state of Texas. It is ironic that when the hurricane hit Galveston later in the year, those same virtues then applied to Houston. (Courtesy of Special Collections, University of Houston Libraries, UH Digital Library.)

A large group of
African American
spectators stands
on the banks of
Buffalo Bayou to
witness a baptism.
Many umbrellas are
present, indicating
an effort to provide
some shade from
the heat of the
day. (Courtesy of
Special Collections,
University
of Houston
Libraries, UH
Digital Library.)

This 1907 postcard shows a section of Buffalo Bayou in downtown Houston. Most of the areas adjacent to the bayou were developed, and the emphasis was on maximizing trade and profit. As this postcard indicates, there was very little concern about natural resources, water quality, or environmental sustainability. (Courtesy of Special Collections, University of Houston Libraries, UH Digital Library.)

In this c. 1900 photograph, people are fishing off a small dam in one of Houston's bayous. The bayous were part of the day-to-day lives of many Houston residents, both for recreation and for sustenance. In undeveloped areas, trees line the banks and are also located along the more stable sandbars. (Courtesy of Special Collections, University of Houston Libraries, UH Digital Library.)

In 1900, the city of Houston purchased the Kellem-Noble land and house on what was then the western edge of town and created the city's first park, Sam Houston Park. The 19-acre park, which is located on the south bank of Buffalo Bayou just west of downtown Houston, was landscaped into a Victorian wonderland, with footpaths laid out to pass by an old mill and cross a rustic bridge over a pleasant stream. (Courtesy of Special Collections, University of Houston Libraries, UH Digital Library.)

Five

1910–1929

BOOMING BUSINESS, RAPID URBANIZATION, AND INCREASING DAMAGE

From 1910 to 1929, business was booming in Houston. The city was growing rapidly, and jobs seemed to be available for anyone who sought one. The urbanization and industrialization of Houston changed the face of the city. The Houston Ship Channel was constructed between 1911 and 1914. The war years (1914–1918) were a time of sacrifice for the country, but in Houston, the ports were busy trying to keep up with demands. The Port of Houston was authorized in 1927, and over the next two years, there were heightened efforts to straighten and clear Buffalo Bayou. For the first time, the Port of Houston began seeking foreign markets in the 1920s.

The federally aided Road Act was enacted in 1916, and it was the first federal highway funding legislation in the United States. In Houston, like in so many other parts of the country, roads were often little more than dirt trails, and during rainstorms they became muddy quagmires. This is especially true of the areas around the bayous, which flooded frequently. The Road Act was a major step in the urbanization of Houston.

In 1915, the Galveston hurricane hit Houston, resulting in $1 million in damages. Other floods occurred throughout this time. Concerns about the impact of urbanization on the bayous continued. For example, raw sewage was routinely drained into the bayou until 1914.

Camp Logan was established along Buffalo Bayou in 1917 and used for training soldiers. In 1925, the city of Houston purchased land that was once Camp Logan and created Memorial Park, and the following year, Eleanor Tinsley Park was also founded.

This period in Houston's history did not end well. Two back-to-back floods in 1929 inundated the city, causing many to question its future. How could it continue to grow and develop if the flooding could not be controlled? Bringing this era to a close was the stock market crash of 1929, which prompted the Great Depression. Although there were shortages in both housing and work, and growth slowed significantly, Houston escaped the most adverse effects of the Depression.

By 1912, Houston's population exceeded 80,000, and there was no end in sight to the growth. The original city limits were expanded to cover 16 square miles, and downtown Houston was dotted with multi-storied office buildings. Streetcars connected the downtown area with adjacent subdivisions, automobiles were commonplace, and 17 rail lines ran in all directions from the city. This photograph is titled "Heart of Houston from Little Franks balloon 1912." (Courtesy of Library of Congress.)

On February 21, 1912, the largest fire in Houston history devastated much of the Fifth Ward, which is the area just north of downtown. Most of the structures in the area were wood frame with wood-shingled roofs, and they offered little resistance to the fire. Fortunately there were no deaths, but more than $3 million in damage was the result. (Courtesy of Library of Congress.)

The 1920s were a decade of change for Houston. The period was a time of urbanization and industrialization, as shown in this 1920 photograph of downtown looking north from the Esperson Building. In 1929, the stock market crashed. (Courtesy of Special Collections, University of Houston Libraries, UH Digital Library.)

Pictured is a barge party on Buffalo Bayou at Morgan's Point with boats of different sizes in the water, including a large barge, a mid-size yacht, and several canoes. A large crowd is gathered on top of the opposite bank, where a train can be seen. (Courtesy of Special Collections, University of Houston Libraries, UH Digital Library.)

MAIN STREET VIADUCT AND SHIP CHANNEL, HOUSTON, TEXAS.

One major issue in the early 1900s was the need for bridges to cross the bayous, especially in the downtown area. By 1913, the Main Street Viaduct connected Main Street on the south side with Montgomery Street on the north side, spanning Buffalo and White Oak bayous and the yards of the Missouri, Kansas & Texas and Houston & Texas Central railways. (Courtesy of Special Collections, University of Houston Libraries, UH Digital Library.)

This 1927 photograph shows the Bayou Bend property of Ima Hogg. The dense growth of the woods along Buffalo Bayou is in contrast to the manicured Diana Garden. Over the years, the wooded edge of the bayou continued to be encroached upon by surrounding development. (Courtesy of Special Collections, University of Houston Libraries, UH Digital Library.)

By 1914, the Ship Channel had been dredged to a depth of 25 feet from the Turning Basin to the Gulf in order to improve navigation. In 1917, the federal government earmarked $3.5 million to deepen the channel to 30 feet, and the work was completed in 1925. The following year, the Port of Houston was ranked 11th in the country in terms of tonnage. This photograph shows the ship channel upstream of Harrisburg. (Courtesy of Special Collections, University of Houston Libraries, UH Digital Library.)

The US Army Corps of Engineers and the Harris County Flood Control District were involved with a number of projects along Buffalo Bayou and its tributaries that focused on flood reduction. These included stream enlargements, clearing, channelization, flood detention basins, diversion channels, and other improvements. (Courtesy of Special Collections, University of Houston Libraries, UH Digital Library.)

In 1917, the War Department established an army training center about five miles west of Houston. The site, called Camp Logan, was located along the northern bank of Buffalo Bayou. In less than two years, the soldiers had all left, and in the mid-1920s—with support from the Hogg family—the city of Houston turned the 1,503-acre site into public open space called Memorial Park. The park is still the largest contiguous undeveloped area along the Buffalo Bayou.

Although some parts of Buffalo Bayou were straightened and cleared in 1927 and 1928, other parts of the bayou were undisturbed. Over the years, these undisturbed areas became more difficult to find because development encroached upon the bayou, and the channel itself was modified in an effort to either improve navigation or reduce flooding. (Courtesy of HCFCD.)

In 1927, the city began clearing and straightening Buffalo Bayou in an effort to improve navigation. In most parts of downtown Houston, native vegetation along the banks of the bayou were removed, and development extended to the edge, or into the bayou channel itself. This 1929 photograph shows work on a concrete bulkhead behind the Henry Henke Ice and Refrigerating Company. (Courtesy of HCFCD.)

The Houston Ship Channel opened in 1914 and has been widened and deepened a number of times since then. Buffalo Bayou is much different than it was when the Allen Brothers made their first trip upstream. The changes to the waterways made Houston a deepwater port variously ranked second or third largest in the United States with access to the shipping of the world. (Courtesy of HCFCD.)

Scenes Taken in Many Sections of City Showing Flood Condition

In April 1929, a massive gulf storm dumped up to 10 inches of rain on parts of Houston, causing extensive flooding along Buffalo Bayou and White Oak Bayou. All bridges over Buffalo and White Oak Bayous west and northwest of the city were underwater. The flood caused more than $1.4 million in damage, with most occurring in the downtown area. A month later, another major storm hit Harris County, and 10 to 15 inches of rain fell over a seven-day period, causing extensive flooding again. The combination of the two storms back to back was devastating to Houston. Flooding had always been an issue along the bayous, but the 1929 storms raised serious concerns about the city's ability to grow until it was better able to reduce flood risks. (Courtesy of the *Houston Chronicle*.)

This photograph shows activity along Houston's ship channel in 1915. The channel was a lively place and was one of the "places to be" in Houston. (Courtesy of Special Collections, University of Houston Libraries.)

In 1912, Harvard-educated landscape architect Arthur C. Comey proposed a comprehensive park system based on Houston's network of bayous. In 1913, he wrote that the "bayous and creek valleys readily lend themselves to trails and parks and cannot so advantageously be used for any other purpose." (Courtesy of City of Houston.)

In the early 1910s, Houston was thriving, and homes, such as these on the corner of Bayland Avenue and Morrison Street, were being developed all across the city. The residential areas closest to the Buffalo Bayou were among the most desirable in the city. (Courtesy of HCFCD.)

In the early 1910s, Houston was one of the most industrialized cities in Texas. The combination of railroad, oil, and shipping industries led to a significant increase in industrial development. These efforts were a result of private entrepreneurship bolstered by government support. (Courtesy of HCFCD.)

When the Allen brothers originally founded Houston, they divided the city into four wards, which were political and geographic districts similar to today's council districts. The city was expanded to include six wards, with the Fifth Ward added in 1866. Originally, freed slaves populated this ward. These types of wooden structures are one reason why the fire of February 21, 1912, which destroyed much of the Fifth Ward, was so devastating. (Courtesy of Special Collections, University of Houston Libraries, UH Digital Library.)

By 1925, Houston had a thriving downtown and all the problems associated with a busy automobile-oriented society. Congestion was a problem, as was noise, air pollution, and water quality. Some of the buildings constructed in this era still stand. (Courtesy of Special Collections, University of Houston Libraries, UH Digital Library.)

This photograph shows a view across the Buffalo Bayou toward the bank. A large yacht with a man standing on the deck is in the center. Other boats are moored nearby. Trees line the bank, and a few buildings are visible on the horizon. (Courtesy of Special Collections, University of Houston Libraries, UH Digital Library.)

In the 1910s and 1920s, Houston became more urbanized and more industrial. Utilities such as electric lines, water lines, and sewer lines were being added, and residential development occurred along the outskirts of the city. This photograph shows Tenth Street near the HTC Railroad crossing. (Courtesy of HCFCD.)

Efforts were made to create an integrated transportation system for Houston and its outlying areas. New streetcar lines were established, older lines were extended, and residents were already making the move to the suburbs by 1907, which was also when construction of a coordinated highway system in Texas was initiated. This photograph, taken at the intersection of Fifth Street and Franklin Street Bridge, shows how transportation was changing within the city. (Courtesy of HCFCD.)

In some sections of downtown Houston, development threatened to choke off Buffalo Bayou. This photograph shows buildings along what was once the Third Street Bridge as seen from the Milam Street Bridge. The scene is just upstream of the confluence of Buffalo and White Oak Bayous. The bridge no longer exists. (Courtesy of HCFCD.)

The Brazos Hotel, which was located across from the Southern Pacific railroad station between Washington Street and Buffalo Bayou, was considered one of the nicest hotels of the time. Sarah Bernhardt, Pres. William Howard Taft, and Pres. Theodore Roosevelt were just a few of the famous guests of the Brazos. The hotel was demolished in 1931 to make way for a Southern Pacific terminal. (Courtesy of HCFCD.)

Buffalo Bayou has a great diversity of flora and fauna along its banks, with some of the more common trees being black willow, box elder, cottonwood, loblolly pine, and sycamore. There are also oaks and hickories in some areas, and native grasses and shrubs create a diverse understory. The vegetation helps stabilize the banks of the bayous. This photograph shows an undeveloped area along Brays Bayou. (Courtesy of HCFCD.)

This photograph shows a World War I homecoming parade on Main Street in 1918. During the war and the years shortly thereafter, the Gulf Coast region provided many of the natural resources needed, and Houston was the hub of distribution efforts. The photograph is labeled "Houston Welcomes 132nd F.A." (Courtesy of Special Collections, University of Houston Libraries, UH Digital Library.)

This photograph shows a panoramic view of the downtown Houston skyline in 1927 looking northeast from a point near Louisiana Street and Lamar Avenue. The Esperson Building, a classic example of Italian Renaissance architecture, is the tallest building in the photograph. When it was constructed in 1927, it dramatically changed Houston's skyline. (Courtesy of Special Collections, University of Houston Libraries, UH Digital Library.)

The Houston Independent School District was established in the 1920s. There were almost 8,900 students in public schools in the district in 1927. In this photograph, temporary buildings were constructed for a school at the intersection of Commerce and Hamilton Streets in Houston. Signs on the building are encouraging people to vote for a new bond to help build new schools. (Courtesy of HCFCD.)

Construction in natural floodplains led to frequent and major flood damage throughout the 1910s and 1920s. Buffalo and White Oak Bayous frequently overflowed their banks, resulting in major floods, especially in the downtown area. Buffalo and White Oak Bayous' back-to-back floods in 1912 and 1913 demonstrated the impact that urbanization was having upon the city. Flooding from another Galveston hurricane in 1915 caused $1 million in damages to Houston. Problems associated with urbanization culminated in the great flood of 1929, when all of the bayous were reported out of their banks. (Courtesy of HCFCD.)

This photograph of a branch of White Oak Bayou west of Woodland Heights illustrates what the landscape was like prior to development. Scattered forests lined the banks, which were stable because of the roots of the trees and established groundcover. Upland grasses slowed down stormwater runoff, so by the time it got to this type of channel, much of the energy of the water had already dissipated. (Courtesy of HCFCD.)

This c. 1910 photograph shows the hustle and bustle of downtown Houston. The wide roadways originally laid out by the Allen Brothers in 1836 proved to be advantageous because they provided sufficient space for traffic, onstreet parking, and wide sidewalks, such as this one on Main Street between Prairie and Texas Avenues. (Courtesy of HCFCD.)

There is an old saying that in Houston, money follows the bayou. The basic idea is that many of the families that settled in Houston did so near Buffalo Bayou, and over the years, these were the families that became wealthy as Houston prospered. Most of these original neighborhoods are still intact and are among the most desirable areas in the city to live. This photograph looks south along Main Street from the corner of Jefferson Avenue. (Courtesy of HCFCD.)

For Houston, the 1920s were an era of prosperity. The city was growing rapidly, the downtown area was the center of commerce, and outdoor booths—like this one at the city market—were commonplace. Bridges and roads were being built, port and railroads expanded, cotton revenues reached new heights, and new construction altered the city's skyline. (Courtesy of HCFCD.)

At the turn of the century, Houston continued to grow, with much of the development occurring along Buffalo Bayou and White Oak Bayou. The original, wide streets as defined by the Allen Brothers allowed taller structures to be built within, creating a sense of confinement or claustrophobia. By 1915, Houston had almost 196 miles of paved streets, and in the following decade, wooden bridges were being replaced with ones of steel and concrete. (Courtesy of HCFCD.)

Six

1930–1939
PROGRESS DESPITE DEPRESSION

After 1929, the Great Depression resulted in tough times across the United States. Economic growth slowed during the early 1930s in Houston, but the city continued to grow, albeit slowly. The state highway system expanded, and Houston roads continued to improve. The automobile quickly dominated the city, but Buffalo Bayou and the Houston Ship Channel were still the driving force behind the city's economy. The Intracoastal Canal system was established in 1934. Houston's economic base became more diverse, and the age of aviation was just getting started. A sign of Houston's maturation is that the city started to show a need for urban renewal.

The Great Flood of 1935 had a major impact on Houston. This flood covered two-thirds of Harris County with water in one day of rainfall. For many, it was the last straw, occurring so soon after the two major floods of 1929. The *Wild River* photographic essay documented the flood of 1935 and was used as the graphic argument to create the Harris County Flood Control District in 1937.

There are several laws that collectively are known as the Flood Control Act. The first, in 1917, focused on controlling floods on the Mississippi, Ohio, and Sacramento Rivers. The 1934 act defined flood control as a legitimate function of the US government, and this led to a major policy change in how flooding was addressed nationwide. Two years later, Congress approved the Federal Flood Control Act of 1936, followed by the Federal Flood Control Act of 1938.

By 1930, Houston was the largest city in Texas with a population of 292,000. The Great Depression slowed the economy, but the city continued to grow. Over the next decade or so, Houston had to learn to deal with many of the problems associated with more mature cities, such as transportation, urban renewal, and sanitation. Industry was becoming a significant factor in the economy, and there were efforts to diversify the economic base.

During the flood of 1935, Buffalo bayou was 52 feet above normal level and seven people were killed. In addition, much of the downtown business district was inundated, as were more than 100 residential blocks. The Houston Ship Channel was partially closed for eight months, and the city's water plant was also shut down. The estimated damage was more than $5 million. (Courtesy of HCFCD.)

Virtually all of downtown Houston was inundated during the flood of 1935. This photograph shows the height of the water and the scale of the disaster. Several buildings collapsed when the waters receded. Not one building in the inundated area escaped damage. (Courtesy of HCFCD.)

The area of Houston around Braes Boulevard near South Main Street was called "Millionaire Row" because of the exclusive homes and estates. During the floods of 1929 and 1935, Brays Bayou overflowed its banks, causing significant damage to the adjacent development. Glenn H. McCarthy, a wealthy oil and hotel man of the time who owned Houston's popular Shamrock Hotel later in the 1940s, also owned the large home in the lower left-hand corner of this photograph.

During the flood of 1935, Buffalo Bayou, which was 52 feet above normal flow, was so high that it almost inundated the Main Street Bridge. Some people sought higher ground, such as the bridges, to stay out of the floodwater. The local paper said it was a miracle that more people were not killed during the flood. (Courtesy of HCFCD.)

In many parts of Houston, the floodwaters of 1935 reached all the way to the second floor. Along Milam Street, floodwaters completely filled the first floors of most buildings. None of the buildings in this part of downtown Houston were undamaged. (Courtesy of HCFCD.)

Downstream from the Hill Street Bridge (now called the Jensen Bridge), much of the area around Buffalo Bayou was still undeveloped in the 1920s and 1930s. The bridge was built in 1938. Today, this landscape is primarily industrial, although it is changing to accommodate a more mixed use because of its proximity to downtown Houston. (Courtesy of HCFCD.)

Severe flooding had occurred along Brays Bayou even before the settlement of Houston. Flooding occurred in the watershed, on average, at least once every decade. As a result, flood damage reduction projects have been implemented along the bayou for years. During this time, the bayou was widened and deepened in places. (Courtesy of HCFCD.)

In this 1939 photograph, barges along Buffalo Bayou are being loaded near Allen's Landing. Although this part of downtown Houston has become more urbanized over the years, the basic infrastructure is much the same as it was in 1939. The San Jacinto Bridge is a visual landmark for the city. (Courtesy of HCFCD.)

A wide variety of boats and barges line the main channel of Brays Bayou. During normal flow, the channel was fairly narrow during this time. Future engineering projects widened and deepened the channel in an effort to make the bayou more accessible and to reduce flooding problems. (Courtesy of HCFCD.)

In the 1930s, there were still areas around eastern Buffalo Bayou and the Port of Houston that were undeveloped, but they were few and far between. The additional growth after World War II cleared out many of these forested areas. (Courtesy of HCFCD.)

"WILD RIVER"
A
PICTORIAL PETITION
PRESENTED TO THE
STATE AFFAIRS COMMITTEES
of the
45th LEGISLATURE
in joint session assembled
at Austin, Texas, March 4th, 1937
URGING FAVORABLE CONSIDERATION OF
Senate Bill Number 114 and
House Bill Number 234

Wild River was a photographic essay prepared by city and county officials with assistance from the Houston Chamber of Commerce and submitted to the Texas legislature on March 4, 1937. The essay tells the story of the Houston flood of 1935 and helped convince the legislature to create the Harris County Flood Control District. (Courtesy of HCFCD.)

As this 1935 photograph of Buffalo Bayou illustrates, erosion has been a persistent problem along the bayou for decades. The steep, soft banks are highly susceptible to erosion. In many places, development along the bayous has led to destabilization of the banks. Development can produce a significant increase in stormwater runoff, loss of vegetation along the bayou banks, and reduced right-of-way, all of which result in increased erosion. (Courtesy of HCFCD.)

This photograph shows how congested Buffalo Bayou could be as a result of all the barges being loaded and the construction along both sides of the bayou. At times there was so much traffic on the bayou that barges had to wait for others to move out of the way before departing. (Courtesy of HCFCD.)

The University of Houston was established in 1926 as a junior college. In 1934, the school was upgraded to a four-year university. This aerial view shows the University of Houston in the foreground with the city in the background. (Courtesy of HCFCD.)

A tug pulls the Regal Beer barge into a dock to be unloaded in this 1935 photograph. Buffalo Bayou was the key to Houston's economic growth, and the addition of the Houston Ship Channel made it easier to bring in shipments from around the country. (Courtesy of HCFCD.)

During the flood of 1935, thousands of people gathered around in downtown Houston to see if buildings, such as city hall, would be impacted by the rising floodwaters. The city hall is only a couple of blocks away from Buffalo Bayou. It was one of many buildings inundated by the flood. (Courtesy of HCFCD.)

The San Jacinto Bridge is a concrete arch bridge that spans Buffalo Bayou. When the bridge was built in 1914, it was hailed for its simple, elegant shape. During construction, it was imperative that the bayou be left open to accommodate boat and barge traffic. The central arch presented an engineering challenge at the time. The bridge is still a visual landmark within the city. (Courtesy of HCFCD.)

The flood of 1935 reached the bottom of the Main Street Viaduct. Other bridges, such as the Capitol Avenue High Bridge, were completely submerged. Traffic in the downtown was disrupted for days, and it took months to repair buildings that were flooded. (Courtesy of HCFCD.)

As a result of the devastating floods that hit the region in 1929 and 1935, the Texas legislature established the Harris County Flood Control District to implement flood damage reduction projects within the county. Since its creation, the district has successfully partnered with the US Army Corps of Engineers on many projects, and throughout the years, the district's partnerships and capabilities have expanded significantly. This photograph shows the first flood control engineers with the district. (Courtesy of HCFCD.)

Among the upper reaches of some of the bayous where development had not resulted in the clearing of adjacent lands, it was still possible to see the natural character of the bayous, even in the 1930s. These bayous provide a glimpse of what they were like when settlers first moved into the area. (Courtesy of HCFCD.)

This photograph shows industry on the banks of the Port of Houston. By the late 1930s, the economy of Houston was booming, and the port was working hard to keep up with demands. As the nation prepared for World War II, the port was busy providing materials and producing products. (Courtesy of HCFCD.)

In this 1939 photograph, a freighter is outbound from the Port of Houston. This particular freighter will load at Galveston, and then the shipment will be taken to its destination. There was a major economic upsurge in the late 1930s as the United States prepared for war. (Courtesy of HCFCD.)

Seven

1940–1969

First Project Plan, Barker and Addicks Reservoirs, World War II, and Postwar Boom Days

The 1940s brought greater diversification to Houston. The Port of Houston expanded to meet demands for World War II and the city completed its first modern airport, built a loop system of roads, and constructed Addicks and Barker Reservoirs in response to the Great Flood of 1935. After the war, there was a shift from war activities to accommodating the demands of a new generation. There was also major growth in urban areas as well as a mass exodus to the suburbs.

In the 1950s and 1960s, Houston was primed for success. With the coming of 1953, *Houston* magazine proclaimed, "Not for many years has America viewed the inauguration of a new year with more optimism. And no other city in the nation has a brighter outlook for a year of great progress than the City of Houston." For the first time, metropolitan Houston passed the million-person mark in population. There was a prolonged drought throughout Texas from 1950 to 1957, but Houston was not impacted as much as the rest of the state.

The city's first expressway, the Gulf Freeway, which connected Houston and Galveston, was opened in 1952. In the late 1950s, the emphasis was on air transportation in Houston, and it was the start of the Space Age. The future space program played an important role in the development of the city. Water became increasingly important due to the increased consumption of both industrial and residential growth.

With the continued growth and urbanization, there were increased development pressures on the bayous. In 1951, a new version of the *Wild River* photo essay was published and was used to help make the argument that the 1940 Comprehensive Plan needed to be updated. The Federal Flood Control Act of 1954 authorized clearing, straightening, enlarging, and lining the channels of Buffalo, White Oak, and Brays Bayous. In 1957, Buffalo Bayou was cleared from Sabine Street to Shepherd Drive. By the end of this period, many of the bayous in the area had been drained, dredged, channelized, or widened. In the 1960s, Terry Hershey and others fought to protect the environmental character of the bayous, starting with stopping the use of concrete channels.

In 1940, the Harris County Flood Control District worked with the US Army Corps of Engineers to develop the first comprehensive flood control plan for Harris County. The 1940 Project Plan included several major projects that focused on routing water around downtown Houston. Three elements of the plan that were completed include: Barker Reservoir (1945), Addicks Reservoir (1948), and the channelization of Buffalo Bayou for six-and-one-fifth miles downstream from Barker Dam (1948). (Courtesy of HCFCD.)

In response to the Great Flood of 1935, Addicks and Barker Reservoirs were constructed to protect areas downstream along Buffalo Bayou and downtown Houston. The reservoirs collect stormwater runoff for western watersheds that drain into Buffalo Bayou, and water is released from the reservoirs into the bayou several times a year as needed. The Addicks and Barker Reservoirs are operated by the US Army Corps of Engineers. When they are dry, the reservoirs are used for active and passive recreational activities. Addicks Reservoir is shown here. (Courtesy Library of Congress, photograph by Carol Highsmith.)

The Yale Street Bridge is a concrete, T-beam bridge that crosses White Oak Bayou between Washington Boulevard and Interstate 10. The bridge was constructed in 1931 and listed in the National Register of Historic Places in 2011. (Courtesy of HCFCD.)

Water hyacinth is an invasive plant that has a significant negative impact on Buffalo Bayou. Invasive plants are species from other parts of the world that, when planted in the Houston-Galveston region, survive, reproduce, and crowd out native plants. Other examples of invasive plants include Chinese tallow and deep-rooted sedge. According to Buffalo Bayou Partnership, a non-profit organization that seeks to protect the bayou, invasive plants and animals cost this country nearly $137 billion annually in economic losses and control costs. (Courtesy of HCFCD.)

Along the upper channel of Buffalo Bayou, a barge is being loaded. Businesses with direct access to the bayous often developed their own private docks to make it easier to load and unload materials. Access roads along the upper banks of the bayou allowed trucks to pull up to the barges. (Courtesy of HCFCD.)

After the end of World War II, construction was booming in Texas. This housing development, which was completed in 1946, is an example of the type of construction projects that were being implemented. Housing was in high demand to accommodate soldiers coming back from the war. (Courtesy of *Life* magazine.)

This image from *Life* magazine shows a powerboat cruising up Buffalo Bayou. After decades of modifications by the US Army Corps of Engineers and the Harris County Flood Control District, much of the bayou can be navigated. Although this photograph suggests that the bayou is green and natural, the majority of it has been straightened and widened over the years, and development encroaches on all sides. (Courtesy of *Life* magazine.)

The Cypress Creek watershed is located in the northwest and north part of Harris County. The creek has wide, extensive floodplains and steep side slopes. The Cypress Creek watershed has also been heavily developed as Houston has grown. (Courtesy of HCFCD.)

Erosion along Buffalo Bayou ranges from common, massive bank failures to smaller-scale toe erosion and localized gully erosion. Typical results are land loss and an undermining of infrastructure. Efforts in the 1940s sought to stabilize slopes and minimize erosion. (Courtesy of HCFCD.)

This photograph shows port facilities at the Barbour Cut Terminal on the Houston Ship Channel. In the foreground are cargo containers that are loaded onto ships and sent to ports worldwide. The Barbour Cut Terminal is a deepwater port. (Courtesy of USACE.)

Many of the tributaries along the bayous were originally small, grass-lined waterways. This tributary runs into Sims Bayou near what is now South Acres Drive. The areas around the tributary have been cleared for agricultural uses and residential development, but the channel itself is still grass-lined, which slows down stormwater runoff. (Courtesy of HCFCD.)

Congress authorized Buffalo Bayou for major flood conveyance improvements with the River and Harbor Act of 1938, modified by the Flood Control Act of 1939, and revised by the Flood Control Act of 1954. Buffalo Bayou was deepened and widened from State Highway 6 to around Rummel Creek by the US Army Corps of Engineers in 1945. (Courtesy of HCFCD.)

The McKee Street Bridge, which was constructed in 1932, has serpentine concrete railings that are supposed to be reminiscent of the waves of Buffalo Bayou. The pastel colors were not applied until the 1980s as part of renovation efforts for the bridge. (Courtesy of the Library of Congress, photograph by Carol Highsmith.)

This photograph shows the underside of the McKee Street Bridge in the early 1940s. The bridge is constructed of concrete girders. At the time of its completion, the McKee Street Bridge was the longest unreinforced concrete bridge in the United States. (Courtesy of the Library of Congress, photograph by Carol Highsmith.)

In the decade after World War II, the Houston economy boomed. Houston was the fastest growing city in the nation, with 76.7 percent growth from 1950 to 1964. The Houston Ship Channel continued to be the lifeline of the city. The advent of air conditioning also had a major impact on the city. In 1953, Houston was considered the most air-conditioned city in the nation, and the luxury was an enticement many companies and individuals needed to make the move to Houston. (Courtesy of HCFCD.)

Page 6, January 2, 1964

Bayou Straightening Work To Begin

Engineer C S Hinshaw shows maps of the plans for rectifying the course of Buffalo Bayou between Huntleigh and Ripple Creek subdivisions.

Rectification of the channel of Buffalo Bayou will begin in the Memorial - Tanglewood area and the Memorial Park area soon after the beginning of the year, according to C S Hinshaw, assistant chief engineer for the Harris County Flood Control office.

Two portions of the bayou, each approximately one and a quarter miles long, will be straightened somewhat and lined with concrete as an erosion control measure, Hinshaw said. Cost of both projects will be about $4 million, and both are expected to be under contract - perhaps even completed - during the coming year.

The design for the channel will fit in with the plans the U S Corps of Engineers has developed for eventual control of flood waters along the bayou, Hinshaw explained.

"There is no particular flooding problem along this bayou," he said, "but there is a serious erosion problem. The Houston Country Club and the River Oaks Country Club have donated rights-of-way at no cost to the district, and in Memorial Park, the Board of Regents of the University of Texas, which controls the property, has also donated right-of-way."

The portion opposite the Houston Country Club extends on the Memorial side approximately from Longwoods to Ripple Creek. Flood control personnel have already showed most property owners plans for the rectification, Hinshaw said.

The channel work will be similar to that along Memorial Drive

Arrows point north; shaded portions will be filled with earth. The channel will be 10 feet wide at the bottom with sloping concrete sides.

between Shepard and downtown, Hinshaw said.

Plans show the concrete-lined ditch to be about feet wide at the bottom, with sloping sides ranging between 18 feet high at Post Oak to 14 feet at Piney Point. Above the level of the concrete, earth fill from the excavations will be placed and graded. The old channel will also be filled to this level where loops are cut off, Hinshaw said.

Property owners along the bayou own to the center of the stream bed, but developers have all been required to dedicate flood control easements. The rights-of-way necessary for erosion control are not necessarily in the same place as the easements, however.

Hinshaw said right-of-way donations enable the flood control

authority to do more work for the money available.

Buffalo Bayou has already been straightened from the dams to Memorial Bend, Hinshaw said, and from Shepherd east to town. He said no timetable has been set up for future work by either the county or the Corps of Engineers along this stream.

"We have to start at the lower end and work up," he explained, "Unfortunately, it's always the upper portions that have floods but we have to have someplace to direct the water first. Then when we ask people lower down for permission to relieve those upstream, they object because they are not experiencing any flooding themselves."

"It's just human nature, I guess," he smiled. "We get used to it."

YWCA Adds 'Law for Layman' Course

Winter term classes for the period through March 7 begin January 13 at the Spring Branch Memorial YWCA, 1102 Campbell Road.

An unusual new course has been added to the general informal education curriculum at the Branch. "Law for the Layman" will be offered on Mondays from 8 to 9 PM. Donald Bevnard, practicing attorney, will discuss practical law including the Texas court system, probate, wills, contracts and taxes.

Other adult courses offered during the winter term are tailoring, sewing, creative dance, antiques, bridge both for beginners and advanced players.

Latin American dancing, according to Mrs. Meda Mason, executive director.

Classes for children start at the three to five-year-old level and range up to teenage activities. Included are creative play school, painting and sketching, sewing, ballroom dancing, a bridge workshop and a course entitled, "You the Charmer," which emphasizes charm and social poise for the teenage girl.

The Branch has expanded its Thrift Shop in which it sells used items to include a Gift Shop serving as a display case and sales vehicle for community painters, sculptors, seamstresses and other artists and craftsmen.

A January 2, 1964, article in the *Baytown Sun* discusses planned channelization work on Buffalo Bayou near Memorial Park. Two portions of the bayou, each approximately one and a quarter miles long, were to be straightened and lined with concrete. The cost of both projects was expected to be around $4 million. This type of approach was consistent with the vision the US Army Corps of Engineers had for the bayous. (Courtesy of the *Baytown Sun*.)

The late 1940s was the greatest building and construction era in the city's history. In December 1948, the Houston City Council approved an ambitious annexation program that dramatically increased the size of the city. The program expanded the city limits from 74.4 square miles to 216 square miles with an estimated population of 620,000. Civic improvement included modern expressways, major storm and sanitary sewer additions, new schools and churches, additional college and university facilities, and extensive hospital expansion programs. (Courtesy of HCFCD.)

In the 1950s, floods were a way of life for those living along the bayous. Every major storm or rainfall could lead to flooding. This 1950 photograph shows a family whose home was flooded when Brays Bayou overflowed its banks. (Courtesy of HCFCD.)

Despite all the modifications to the bayous, flooding was still a problem when these photographs were taken in 1950. To help provide funding for new flood damage reduction plans, civic leaders prepared a 1951 version of *Wild River* to highlight existing flooding issues. The document was similar to the 1937 edition in some ways, but in addition to downtown Houston, it included the Ship Channel and Brays Bayou. The primary argument of the document was that Houston would not be able to continue to grow and develop unless flooding issues were addressed. The 1951 *Wild River* was part of the call for a revision to the 1940 Project Plan, which was viewed as being somewhat effective but also lacking in terms of environmental and aesthetic concerns. (Courtesy of HCFCD.)

Since the 1950s, several natural streams in Harris County were channelized and lined with concrete to increase the flow of water during storm events. The purpose was to reduce flooding. One major negative impact, however, is that native vegetation was removed, wildlife habitat devastated, and the "green" feel of the bayous was destroyed. This photograph shows a US Army Corps of Engineers project for Brays Bayou that straightened the channel, removed riparian vegetation, and added a concrete channel. (Courtesy of HCFCD.)

This 1966 photograph shows the finished concrete channel for Brickhouse Gully. These utilitarian approaches to stormwater management may have been effective from an engineering standpoint, but they were a major source of irritation for those concerned about the impact these types of solutions have upon environmental resources and community character. Public pressure in the late 1960s and early 1970s stopped the implementation of concrete channels along the bayous. (Courtesy of HCFCD.)

Over time, nearly all of the bayous draining Harris County have been altered to improve drainage and to provide additional stormwater conveyance. This photograph of White Oak Bayou demonstrates the kind of flood damage reduction projects that were being constructed in Harris County during the 1950s and 1960s. These projects focused on the utility of stormwater management without placing much concern on environmental, cultural, or visual resources. (Courtesy of the Library of Congress, photograph by Carol Highsmith.)

This 1945 photograph shows the US Navy Cleveland-class cruiser USS *Houston* cruising down Buffalo Bayou on its way to Galveston Bay. This was the third vessel in the US Navy named after the city of Houston. It was decommissioned on December 15, 1947. (Courtesy of HCFCD.)

In 1954, Congress approved new flood damage reduction plans for many of the bayous around Houston. These plans involved clearing out existing vegetation, straightening and widening channels, and creating engineering slopes that maximized flood management. This photograph shows construction of a typical engineering solution for Brays Bayou. By the 1960s, many residents along Buffalo Bayou objected to channelization plans for aesthetic and environmental reasons. After the White Oak and Brays projects were completed, work on the 1954 plan ceased. (Courtesy of HCFCD.)

In the decade after World War II, a number of petrochemical industries set up business along the Houston Ship Channel. The last vacant suitable land for docks and warehouses along the channel was sold for development. This illustration shows activities at the Turning Basin. (Courtesy of Special Collections, University of Houston Libraries, UH Digital Library.)

In 1957, a monorail was constructed in Houston as part of a study to see how best to address the city's transportation issues. The monorail was located in Houston's Arrowhead Park. Unfortunately, it only lasted eight months or so before it was dismantled. It does indicate, though, the progressive attitude that the city had in terms of planning for the future. (Courtesy of *Life* magazine.)

Eight

1970–1990:
Environmental Concerns Amidst a Booming Economy, and the Dark Days of the Recession

The National Environmental Policy Act of 1970 is one of the most important pieces of legislation of this century and has a significant impact on every project in the United States that requires federal funding or permitting, including the bayous of Houston. In 1972, the Houston Ship Channel received the dubious honor of being labeled one of the "filthiest bodies of water in the country." In 1975, 10.7 miles of White Oak Bayou was channelized and lined with concrete. Because of efforts of Terry Hershey, George H.W. Bush, and others, the 1954 flood damage reduction plan was stopped. Hershey's efforts lead to an alternative plan being developed for the upper part of Buffalo Bayou, and the area has a green, park-like setting defined by forested habitat on both sides of the channel.

Houston became a world energy capital in the 1970s, but there was a concentrated effort to continue the diversification of the economic base to broaden the range of businesses. While the rest of the country was dealing with a severe recession in 1975, Houston continued to thrive. Growth patterns would change, though. A survey of new office buildings in 1981 revealed that more new office space was built in the suburbs than was built downtown during the preceding five years. The economic problems of the 1980s were similar to those of the Great Depression. In the late 1980s, Houston was hit hard by the drop in oil prices, and for the first time the city declined in population.

In 1979, seven separate flood events occurred within the city. In August 1983, Hurricane Alicia struck Galveston and Harris County, resulting in extensive flooding along all area bayous and streams and causing nearly $1 billion in damage. Other flood events continued throughout this time.

In 1988, the US Army Corps of Engineers completed the Buffalo Bayou and Tributaries Study and determined that work on Brays Bayou would help reduce flooding. This led to development of the Brays Bayou Federal Flood Damage Reduction Project. Buffalo Bayou Park was created in the early 1980s; it was later renamed to honor Terry Hershey.

Increased urbanization in Harris County has led to the loss of some of the forested areas within the county. As a result, there was increased interest in the late 1960s and early 1970s to take a more natural approach to stormwater management and to protect existing vegetation and habitat surrounding the bayous. These photographs are of Greens Bayou. (Courtesy of HCFCD.)

In the early 1970s, 10.7 miles of channel improvements were completed along White Oak Bayou. In response, local citizens led by Bayou Preservation Association founding member Terry Hershey and supported by Congressman George H.W. Bush fought against similar changes to Buffalo Bayou. As a result, plans to straighten and use concrete lining on Buffalo Bayou were abandoned. (Courtesy of J. Sipes.)

Buffalo Bayou Park was created in 1985 and later renamed Terry Hershey Park in 1991 as a result of her efforts to develop an alternative plan for the bayou. The park has more than 500 acres of public open space; within the park, the bayou has a fairly natural look and feel that includes trails, recreation amenities, wildlife habitat areas, and natural areas. (Courtesy of J. Sipes.)

Greens Bayou has been a major focus of efforts to implement engineering solutions for flood damage reduction. In February 1950, a series of thunderstorms resulted in more than six inches of rainfall, and Greens Bayou wound up running out of its banks. Many area residents were evacuated. This event was typical of the types of flooding that would occur along Greens Bayou. Major flooding events happened in 1949, 1957, 1964, 1966, and 1973. The Greens Bayou Wetlands Mitigation Bank was implemented in the early 1990s to address environmental concerns along the bayou, and it is still being used today. (Courtesy of HCFCD.)

This cross-section shows an example of how Buffalo Bayou could be developed to accommodate multiple uses. To the far left are upland forests, which include linear bio-retention basins. These basins collect and treat stormwater runoff before it flows into the bayou. Native vegetation helps stabilize the steep banks of the bayou. Trails along the top of the banks provide access for pedestrians to access the bayou. (Courtesy of J. Sipes.)

In the 1970s, there was much debate about the importance of environmental issues when it came to major transportation and water management projects. In 1977, House Majority Leader Jim Wright of Texas said the environmental movement "has taken on some of the foolish aspects of a fad and a great deal of mischief has been done in the process. It is time to separate the serious from the silly. We have been on a binge of emotion and a drought of common sense." Many did not agree with Wright's statement. This is a photograph of Greens Bayou and the Greens Bayou Wetlands Mitigation Bank. (Courtesy of HCFCD.)

In the early 1970s, water pollution was getting a lot of attention. Houston was identified as the biggest single polluter, and the Ship Channel was often mentioned as the most polluted body of water in the country. Inadequate and overloaded sewage treatment plants were a major reason, and stormwater runoff washed pollutants directly into the bayous. A new sewage treatment plant on Buffalo Bayou was completed in 1983. (Courtesy of J. Sipes.)

This photograph shows Little White Oak Bayou, one of the many tributaries that run into White Oak Bayou. The channel and banks are paved with concrete to improve stormwater runoff and reduce flooding in adjacent neighborhoods. The result is a tributary that seems more like a drainage ditch than a natural waterway. (Courtesy of HCFCD.)

Buffalo Bayou is one of the largest bayous in Harris County. This photograph shows the bayou after a fairly normal rainfall in 2011. The bayou has always flooded to some degree, but as the watershed become more urbanized, flooding became more of a problem. As a general rule, an increase in the amount of paving in a watershed also increases the intensity of flooding. In Houston, this has been an ongoing problem. (Courtesy of J. Sipes.)

This 1980 photograph shows downtown Houston as seen from the nearby University of Houston. Buffalo Bayou can be seen in the foreground. In the 1980s, there was more interest in integrating the bayou as an overall part of community character. (Courtesy of the Library of Congress, photograph by Carol Highsmith.)

Deregulation of railroads occurred in the early 1980s, and between 1980 and 1999, there was a significant consolidation of railroads to create bigger, more powerful companies. Houston got a new passenger train service in 1989, but commuter rail proposals were controversial and did not achieve the level of support needed for implementation. (Courtesy of the Library of Congress, photography by Carol Highsmith.)

This photograph shows Buffalo Bayou as it weaves through downtown Houston. The bayou is at a high level as a result of recent rainstorms, but it is staying within its banks. The level of water in the bayous varies considerably; during hot summer months, it can be quite low. (Courtesy of HCFCD.)

This photograph shows Buffalo Bayou Park with downtown Houston in the background. The statue, called the *Large Spindle Piece*, was created by British sculptor Henry Moore in 1969 and is located on a prominent grass knoll between Allen Parkway and Memorial Drive. (Courtesy of the Library of Congress, photography by Carol Highsmith.)

This interpretive sign was developed via a partnership between the Houston Parks and Recreation Department and the Harris County Flood Control District. The sign, which is located along the bayous, highlights the roles that wetlands play in stormwater management. Not only do they provide benefits by naturally cleaning stormwater, they also benefit area wildlife. (Courtesy of HCFCD.)

At Art Storey Park, the wetland areas provide valuable habitat for a variety of species. Over the years, as the bayous have been widened, dredged, and channelized, thousands of acres of wildlife habitat were destroyed. Efforts, like Art Storey Park, seek to reverse that trend by not only protecting existing natural resources, but also creating new habitat areas. (Courtesy of HCFCD.)

Storage tanks for petrochemical products can be seen in this aerial photograph. Despite the drop in oil prices during the 1970s and 1980s, Houston is still very much dependent upon petroleum-based products. As long as Texas is an oil state, the Port of Houston will be shipping it to other parts of the country. (Courtesy of the Library of Congress, photography by Carol Highsmith.)

This 1980 photograph shows one of the many subdivisions in Houston. Much more so than most major cities, Houston is very spread out. The majority of the city is very low density, and only certain areas, like the Energy Corridor, the Galleria, Downtown Houston, and a few other development clusters, are fairly dense. (Courtesy of the Library of Congress, photography by Carol Highsmith.)

This photograph shows how development has encroached upon Spring Branch, a tributary of Buffalo Bayou. The townhouses on the southwest side of the bayou come all the way up to the top of the bayou's bank, as does the office building on the northeast side. The natural flood plains of the bayou have been filled in with this type of development. (Courtesy of HCFCD.)

Because of the flat terrain, when it rains heavily in Houston, it typically floods. Some of the flooding occurs when the bayous overflow. Flooding also occurs because rainwater falling in outer areas of a watershed is not able to get to the bayous and creeks. Development has exacerbated this type of secondary flooding. (Courtesy of HCFCD.)

This photograph shows the land uses around Brays Bayou. The bayou has been straightened and widened over the years, and much of the native vegetation along the banks has been removed. In the upper-right corner is Art Storey Park under construction. (Courtesy of HCFCD.)

This photograph shows Sims Bayou as it meanders through the southern part of the city. The first bridge (in the lower part of the photograph) is Broadway, and the second bridge shows Interstate 45, also called the Gulf Freeway. The meandering channel is engineered to slow down the flow of water and protect against erosion. After many severe rainstorms, flooding has been reduced along the newly configured bayou. (Courtesy of HCFCD.)

This photograph shows a 110-acre detention basin on Sims Bayou. These types of basins are used to accommodate floodwater when the bayou overflows. The floodwater is directed to the basins, where it spreads out and loses energy; it is then slowly released back to the bayou once the peak of a flood dissipates. (Courtesy of HCFCD.)

Nine

1991–1999:
ENVIRONMENTAL CONSTRAINTS AND ENGINEERING INNOVATION

By the early 1990s, emphasis in Houston had shifted from expansion to management of the existing city. Urban renewal was a high priority.

In the 1990s, many of the bayous of Houston and their associated floodplains were impacted by continuing development and flood damage reduction projects. The Houston metropolitan area was still growing and this growth resulted in additional stress on the bayous and their storm drainage function. The Harris County Flood Control District continued major flood damage reduction planning and construction programs within the Brays Bayou, White Oak Bayou, Hunting Bayou, Buffalo Bayou, Sims Bayou, Clear Creek, Greens Bayou, and Halls Bayou watersheds. Additionally, some civic activities helped improve the aesthetics of and access to some of the bayous. For example, Sesquicentennial Park was completed in 1998 by the Buffalo Bayou Partnership, and trails were expanded significantly in Terry Hershey Park by Harris County Precinct 3.

A September 25, 1996, article by the Associated Press reported, "Texas water filled with toxins; More than 28.8 million pounds of toxic chemicals were legally dumped by industrial facilities into Texas waterways over a five-year period, and nearly two-thirds of that went into the Houston Ship Channel, a new study says. The study covers 1990 through 1994."

In March 1992, a major storm flooded more than 1,500 residences and businesses in Houston, and many bayous were out of their banks. In 1994, a major storm inundated Southeast Texas, dumping 4 to 29 inches of rain in three days over Harris County alone. Countywide, nearly 3,400 residences in 90 subdivisions were flooded. In September 1998, Tropical Storm Frances caused extensive flooding in Harris County along White Oak Bayou and other bayous. More than 1,300 residences were flooded, and much of the downtown area was also flooded.

This portion of Brays Bayou runs through the Houston Medical Center. Much of the bayou has been channelized over the years, and the watershed itself is almost all urbanized. Channelization work on 25.4 miles of Brays Bayou was completed in 1968. (Courtesy of HCFCD.)

During and following storm events, the US Army Corps of Engineers regulates Buffalo Bayou's flow below Addicks and Barker Reservoirs, resulting in higher sustained flows and altered sediment transport while the reservoir drains. The embankments for the reservoirs clearly separate them from adjacent commercial development. (Courtesy of US Army Corps of Engineers.)

Some of the wetlands along the bayous have been protected over the years despite all of the engineering changes that have occurred. The Radney Road wetlands along Buffalo Bayou is an example of a wetland area within the fully urbanized Buffalo Bayou watershed. (Courtesy of J. Sipes.)

Project Brays uses a collaborative approach with multiple techniques to address flood risks. The three major techniques being used are channel modifications, bridge modifications, and the construction of regional stormwater detention basins. Major benefits of Project Brays are that it helps create new public spaces, protects existing natural resources, and creates new natural areas. (Courtesy of HCFCD.)

Despite the level of urbanization along many of the bayous, there are still valuable habitat areas in the most unlikely places. This photograph shows a yellow crowned night heron enjoying the quiet of a small lagoon behind the Hidden Lake Townhomes off of White Oak Bayou. (Courtesy of C. Stull.)

White Oak Bayou has been heavily engineered over the years. A concrete-lined channel, steep engineered slopes, and a trail along each side exemplify much of the bayou. There are multi-use trails along both sides of it in many locations. (Courtesy of US Army Corps of Engineers.)

The National Aeronautics and Space Administration chose Houston for its Manned Spacecraft Center, and the Johnson Space Center was completed in the late 1960s. Houston became known as Space City, and the famous line from the Apollo 13 mission, "Houston, we have a problem," is one of the more memorable quotes of a generation. This photograph shows the space center in 1969. Clear Lake can be seen in the background. (Courtesy of Wikipedia Commons.)

The Arthur Storey Park Stormwater Detention Basin is one of four storm water detention basins completed by Project Brays. It is the second-largest storm water detention basin within the project and also provides 210 acres of much-needed public space for Harris County. The basin holds approximately 1.1 billion gallons of stormwater, greatly reducing potential flooding downstream. (Courtesy of HCFCD.)

When Arthur Storey Park was constructed along the Arthur Storey Park Stormwater Detention basin in 1997, it was applauded for how it addressed flood damage reduction. The project blends stormwater detention with a park environment so that it not only reduces potential flooding issues, but also creates a public amenity. This is a dramatic departure from how flood damage reduction used to be addressed in the Houston area. Every weekend, hundreds of Harris County residents visit the park to take advantage of the trails and other recreational opportunities. These trails are inundated during major floods. (Courtesy of HCFCD.)

The Arthur Storey Park Stormwater Detention Basin includes recreational amenities, such as trails, ponds, and even a Tai Chi court. It also incorporates natural features, like a large grove of trees and wetlands that provide wildlife habitat for a number of species. (Courtesy of HCFCD.)

This is one of several detention basins along White Oak Bayou. The basin is designed to handle overflow from the bayou during flooding events. Most of the White Oak bayou watershed is urbanized, and the increase in pavement has exacerbated flooding problems in the area. (Courtesy of HCFCD.)

The inline weir along White Oak Bayou (above) is used to slow down the velocity of water and reduce the level of energy. The Sims Bayou Federal Flood Damage Reduction Project is a partnership project between the US Army Corps of Engineers and the Harris County Flood Control District. The project includes 19.3 miles of bayou enlargements and environmental enhancements. To armor the banks of the bayou, the project uses articulated concrete blocks rather than a solid concrete lining. The blocks have openings that allow grass and other vegetation to grow. (Both, courtesy of HCFCD.)

At Terry Hershey Park, located along Buffalo Bayou, a series of terraced, linear detention basins are used to accommodate stormwater overflow when water runs over the banks of the bayou. Trails are located along the outside edges of the basins, and forested areas are protected to help maintain the park-like setting. The project included bank erosion protection as well as preservation and enhancement of the riparian corridor. (Courtesy of HCFCD.)

Within Terry Hershey Park, the landscape has been carved to create linear bio-retention basins that run parallel to Buffalo Bayou. The lower parts of the basins get inundated when the bayou floods. In this photograph, the bayou is to the right, and residential neighborhoods are to the left. (Courtesy of HCFCD.)

Along many of the bayous, the channels have been widened and cleared, but native vegetation grows along the banks. Some of this vegetation is relatively unchanged, but much of it is fairly recent and has been re-established after the banks were modified. This photograph shows an upper reach of Buffalo Bayou. (Courtesy of J. Sipes.)

In the parts of the bayous that have not been overly engineered, the habitat has recovered with new vegetation. In these areas, there are a variety of birds, mammals, and aquatic species as well as a broad combination of fauna. Invasive species are a problem in many parts of the bayous, however. (Courtesy of HCFCD.)

Ten

2000–PRESENT
THE BAYOU AND HOUSTON'S COMMERCIAL BOOM

Despite all of the changes to the bayous, a major flood still occurs somewhere in Harris County about every two years. Tropical Storm Allison in 2001 was one of the most devastating rain events in the history of the United States. Two million people were affected, over 70,000 residences were flooded, and 22 people lost their lives. Total damage exceeded $5 billion. In October and November 2002, nine straight days of rainfall flooded White Oak, Greens, and Halls Bayous, and more than 2,000 homes were flooded. In June 2006, eleven inches of rainfall led to more than 3,000 homes being flooded in several watersheds. A major storm in April 2009 flooded more than 900 homes along Buffalo Bayou. Even in good weather, water-quality testing has found that bacteria concentrations are elevated in the bayous, posing a risk for people who come in contact with the water.

A number of innovate projects were implemented along the bayous. Since 1994, Project Brays has primarily focused on the construction of four major stormwater detention basins as well as channel modifications. The total cost of Project Brays will be approximately $450 million. In 2000, linear detention basins were constructed in the upper reach of Buffalo Bayou at Terry Hershey Park. In 2001, a new funding approach of HCFCD provided significantly more money for flood damage reduction projects. In 2005, The Buffalo and Lower White Oak Federal Study began, evolving into Charting Buffalo, which sought to integrate community enhancement opportunities. A similar federal study was initiated for Halls Bayou in 2006. The 2006 Brays Bayou Tidal Marsh Project and Greens Bayou Wetlands Mitigation Bank are two projects that combined wetland creation, mitigation, and natural stormwater runoff treatment.

How will Houston interact with its bayous in the future? There need to be more efforts to rebuild the ecological balance of the bayou's natural environments. "All our 2,500 miles of bayous are important to people and habitat, just as they were for the Allen brothers when they founded Houston on the banks of Buffalo Bayou," said Kathy Lord, executive director of the Bayou Preservation Association in a November 19, 2010, article in the *Houston Chronicle*.

The Texas Medical Center is the largest medical center in the world. It contains 50 medicine-related institutions, including 15 hospitals and two specialty institutions. It was established in 1945, and the impact of the center on Houston's economy has been significant. Not all of the center's institutions are in Houston; the ones that are occupy a 1,000-acre site near the downtown area. (Courtesy of the Library of Congress, photography by Carol Highsmith.)

There are still debates about the concrete-lined channel along portions of White Oak Bayou. Some want the concrete removed and replaced with a more natural grass bottom with the steep, engineering slopes being regraded and revegetated to create a more environmentally sustainable landscape. (Courtesy of HCFCD.)

In some locations, the banks of Buffalo Bayou are very steep and have experienced severe erosion over the years. As the volume and velocity of water coming down the channel during heavy rainstorms increases, the likelihood of steep banks collapsing also increases. (Courtesy of J. Sipes.)

This photograph shows a section of Hunting Bayou near US 59. The watershed is highly urbanized with a mixture of residential, commercial, and industrial developments. The bayou is just northeast of downtown Houston and runs adjacent to Buffalo Bayou. The Hunting Hike and Bike Trail is about one mile long and runs parallel to the bayou. (Courtesy of J. Sipes.)

The suspension walking bridge over Buffalo Bayou connects to Bayou Bend, which is the former home of Houston philanthropist and collector Ima Hogg. The bridge is popular among visitors because it offers views of the bayou, and the movement of the bridge adds a level of excitement. (Courtesy of J. Sipes.)

The Edith L. Moore Nature Sanctuary in West Houston is a 17.5-acre wooded sanctuary along Rummel Creek, a tributary of Buffalo Bayou. Houston Audubon, a chapter of the National Audubon Society, manages the site. The mission of the sanctuary is to provide an urban wildlife sanctuary for native plants and animals and offer environmental education opportunities. (Courtesy of J. Sipes.)

Before the settlement of Houston in 1836, the bayous in the area naturally flooded. Because of the relatively flat terrain, impervious soils, narrow channels, and intense rainfalls, when it rained, the bayous flooded. The problem is that this naturally occurring event was no longer acceptable once people started settling along the banks of the bayous. (Courtesy of Depositphotos.)

In the last few years, downtown Houston has undergone significant urban renewal. The sign of a mature city is that it expands to a point where renovation is required. This photograph of the downtown area is just one block south of Buffalo Bayou. Development of the bayou and development of downtown are linked. (Courtesy of J. Sipes.)

This playground is part of Terry Hershey Park. The recreational space includes a parking lot, trails, wayfinding signage, and restroom facilities, and it functions as a trailhead to access the paths in the rest of Terry Hershey Park. (Courtesy of HCFCD.)

Trails line both sides of Buffalo Bayou in many locations, and these types of pedestrian underpasses allow people and bicyclists to travel under roadways safely. The bayou is visible along the left of the photograph. This underpass connects the trailhead off Memorial Drive with the rest of the trails in the park. (Courtesy of J. Sipes.)

The Rosemont Bridge, Houston's newest pedestrian bridge, provides access across Buffalo Bayou to the Buffalo Bayou Park. The 780-foot-long bridge is composed of seven structural sections that were lifted and placed on a set of piers in order to minimize environmental impact. Kevin Shanley, CEO for the SWA Group, which designed the bridge, said, "Its striking visual presence, beautiful columns, railings, and truss structure are reminiscent of freeways, which is very appropriate for Houston." (Courtesy of J. Sipes.)

This photograph shows the outfall from the Barker Reservoir. Banks of the channel leading from the reservoir are either engineered slopes or paved with hardscape and blocks that allow vegetation to grow. When the reservoir is open, this channel will be full of floodwater. (Courtesy of J. Sipes.)

This is one of many docks along Buffalo Bayou and the ship channel. This one is located near the Buffalo Bayou Oxbow. The docks are used to load and unload products that are either being delivered or getting ready to be shipped to other parts of the world. Many of the docks have been operational for more than a century. (Courtesy of HCFCD.)

The section of Buffalo Bayou that runs through downtown Houston has undergone a number of changes over the years. Banks on both sides of the bayou have been engineered through this section, and trails provide access along the bayou. The building in the distance is the Harris County jail facility. (Courtesy of J. Sipes.)

A landmark is established downtown at the confluence of Buffalo Bayou and White Oak Bayou. The original settlement of Houston was established in this area and has grown outward ever since. The building straight ahead is the Harris County jail facility. (Courtesy of HCFCD.)

In the last two decades, there has been a greater emphasis on reestablishing the environmental functions of the bayous. This wetland on Radney Road off Buffalo Bayou is an example of how natural systems can be beneficial in controlling flooding, providing wildlife habitat, and addressing water quality. (Courtesy of J. Sipes.)

This photograph was taken from inside one of the concrete culverts leading into a creek that flows into Buffalo Bayou. The steep banks are unstable in some places, while large rock has been placed along other parts of the banks in order to minimize erosion, which causes severe siltation problems in the bayou. (Courtesy of HCFCD.)

The Buffalo Bayou and Sesquicentennial Park is a 10.4-acre site along Buffalo Bayou where it passes in front of the Wortham Center. The park was developed as a commemoration of Houston's and Texas's 150th birthday. The steps in the middle of the photograph lead down to a lower level that runs parallel to the bayou. (Courtesy of HCFCD.)

Along the eastern bank and against the Wortham Center are seven 70-foot-tall stainless steel pillars designed by artist Mel Chin called *The Seven Wonders*. Sesquicentennial Park is a unique venue for outdoor activities of all kinds, such as the Buffalo Bayou Regatta and other events that involve public gatherings. (Courtesy of Depositphotos.)

The confluence of Buffalo and White Oak Bayous is a place of importance in Houston history. This is where the Allen brothers defined the center of Houston, and it was an important dock for loading and unloading barges during the early years of the city. In recent years, there have been efforts to emphasize this part of the city for tourism. The photograph above shows the view from the ground, while the aerial view below provides a broader context for how the bayous come together. (Above, courtesy of J. Sipes; below, courtesy of HCFCD.)

In recent years, there has been more of an emphasis on the visual and environmental quality of the bayous. More than 175 years of development has resulted in many of the bayous looking more engineered than natural. In the last decade, a number of new projects have been developed along the bayous to make Houston more "green." (Courtesy of HCFCD.)

Homeless people live under bridges west of downtown Houston. Like many other cities, Houston is trying to figure out the best way to accommodate the needs of the homeless while also continuing efforts to clean up the waterfront and promote tourism along Buffalo Bayou. (Courtesy of J. Sipes.)

Downtown Houston was completely inundated by floodwater resulting from Tropical Storm Allison. The photograph above shows the flooding that occurred where Buffalo and White Oak Bayous come together near Main Street. Below, the floods that resulted from Tropical Storm Allison covered parts of Interstate 45, such as at this location near Wrightwood Street just north of White Oak Boulevard near downtown Houston. I-45 was just one of many major roadways that had to be closed down because of the floods. (Courtesy of HCFCD.)

It was estimated that more than 77,000 automobiles were trapped by the floodwaters that resulted from Tropical Storm Allison. The floodwaters rose so quickly that some motorists were caught off guard. Others decided to plow through the water, not realizing how deep it was. Some motorists made it, but most did not. More than 73,000 homes were flooded as a result of the storm. Many residents had to leave their homes for weeks. After the floodwaters subsided, many of the homes were found to have mold as a result of the floodwaters. (Courtesy of HCFCD.)

Allison completely flooded downtown Houston, including the underground tunnel system that serves as a pedestrian way linking many of the large office buildings in the area. The tunnel system has since been upgraded to prevent similar floods in the future. (Courtesy of HCFCD.)

Tropical Storm Allison dropped 15 inches or more over 2,180 square miles, which is more than three times the area of the city of Houston. Detention basins were completely full and could not handle all of the stormwater runoff. When the storm was finally over, more than 35 inches of rain had fallen as a result of Allison. (Courtesy of HCFCD.)

119

Stude Park is just north of White Oak Bayou between Studemont and Taylor Streets, north of downtown Houston. This is one of the few parts of White Oak Bayou that is easily accessible to the public, but the channel itself is concrete-lined and not really viewed as a community asset because of its lack of environmental and aesthetic integrity. (Courtesy of HCFCD.)

This photograph shows early construction work as part of the Sims Bayou Federal Flood Damage Reduction Project. The project includes 19.3 miles of bayou enlargements and environmental enhancements along Sims Bayou from the Houston Ship Channel to Croquet Street. It costs somewhere around $379 million. (Courtesy of HCFCD.)

Buffalo Bayou is a major source of recreation for these canoeists and kayakers. The 39th annual Buffalo Bayou Regatta included more than 400 participants. The event, sponsored by the Buffalo Bayou Partnership, is the state's largest canoe and kayak race. The 15-mile race is a USCA-sanctioned event. (Courtesy of HCFCD.)

Spring Creek runs west to east on the north side of the city and drains to the San Jacinto River, which in turn drains into Lake Houston. It is a popular recreation area for canoeists. In addition, a 10-mile greenway trail runs parallel to the creek, connecting Pundt Park in Spring, Texas, to the Jesse H. Jones Park and Nature Center in Humble. (Courtesy of HCFCD.)

Over the course of 175 years, there have been a lot of changes to the bayous. One problem is that the construction of new bridges and roads had a negative environmental impact on the bayous. In this photograph of Buffalo Bayou near Dairy Ashford Road, the piers of bridges are constructed directly in the channel bottom. The environmental impacts of both the construction and the current location of the piers is a significant concern. (Courtesy of HCFCD.)

The 7,800-acre George Bush Park, named for Pres. George H.W. Bush, is located on the far west side of Houston near Westheimer Parkway. The park serves as a major attraction and nature reserve and includes a series of trails that follow Buffalo Bayou. It also has swamps, forest, bayous, and other natural resources that help define the overall character of the park. (Courtesy of Wikipedia Commons.)

The Willow Waterhole Stormwater Detention Basin is one of the four large stormwater detention basins that are part of Project Brays. Upon completion, the basin will hold approximately 600 million gallons of stormwater. The greenway surrounding the basin is a popular recreational space as well. (Courtesy of HCFCD.)

In recent years, land has been acquired along Brays Bayou as part of Project Brays, which consists of more than 70 individual projects throughout the entire 31 miles of Brays Bayou. The objective of Project Brays is to provide community open space, protect water quality, reduce the potential for flood damage, and enhance wildlife habitat. This photograph shows the Brays Bayou Marsh at Mason Park, which was completed in 2006. (Courtesy of HCFCD.)

The Buffalo Bayou Promenade is a 23-acre urban park situated along Buffalo Bayou near downtown Houston. The 1.2-mile long promenade links Buffalo Bayou Park to the west with Houston's Theater District and the downtown area. Traditionally, development had turned its back on this portion of the bayou, which was littered with trash, debris, and silt. The promenade creates a linear park that takes what was once wasted space and transforms it into landscaped spaces with trails and walkways. The success of the park has spurred similar improvements along other parts of the bayous. (Courtesy of HCFCD.)

The Rosemont Bridge over Buffalo Bayou is part of a larger $55 million plan by Buffalo Bayou Partnership to overhaul 158 acres of parkland along Buffalo Bayou west of downtown. These types of projects not only show how to develop public green space along the bayou and protect environmental resources, they also illustrate how public and private partnerships can lead to successful results. (Courtesy of J. Sipes.)

This graphic display shows different landscape restoration approaches that can be applied to flood damage reduction projects along the bayous. The objective is to create a more sustainable natural environment. (Courtesy of J. Sipes.)

The Sabine Street Bridge crosses Buffalo Bayou just west of I-45. The bridge was built in 1924 and improved in 1987, and is listed in the National Register of Historic Places. It marks the eastern boundary of Buffalo Bayou Park, and together the bridge and park exemplify the integration of past and future.

Potential wet-bottom detention basins along the bayous could include raised boardwalks that allow pedestrians to take advantage of the attractive setting. This type of approach to flood damage reduction could also help provide wildlife habitat, improve aesthetics, and provide opportunities for passive recreation. (Courtesy of J. Sipes.)

BIBLIOGRAPHY

Aulbach, Louis F. "Buffalo Bayou: An Echo of Houston's Wilderness Beginnings." users.hal-pc.org/~lfa/Buffalo.html.

George Fuermann "Texas and Houston" Collection. Texas Archival Resources Online. www.lib.utexas.edu/taro/uhsc/00027/hsc-00027.html.

Green, James B. "Flood Control and Drainage in Harris County." *Houston Engineer*. April 1980.

"Scenes Taken in many Sections of City Showing Flood Condition." *The Houston Chronicle*. June 1, 1929.

Wild River. A pictorial petition presented to the State Affairs Committees of the 45th legislatures. Austin, Texas: March 4, 1937.

"Buffalo Bayou." Wikipedia. en.wikipedia.org/wiki/Buffalo_Bayou
Buffalo Bayou Partnership. www.buffalobayou.org
Harris County Flood Control District. www.hcfcd.org
Houston History. houstonhistorymagazine.org
Newspaper Archive. www.newspaperarchive.com
Project Brays. www.projectbrays.org
Texas State Historical Association. www.tshaonline.org
University of Houston Digital Library. digital.lib.uh.edu

Visit us at
arcadiapublishing.com

CPSIA information can be obtained
at www.ICGtesting.com
Printed in the USA
LVHW062135071119
636735LV00016B/165/P